Fill'er Up

QUILTING DESIGNS

RENAE HADDADIN

American Quilter's Society

P.O. Box 3290 • Paducah, KY 42002-3290
Fax 270-898-1173 • e-mail: orders@AQSquilt.com

Located in Paducah, Kentucky, the American Quilter's Society (AQS) is dedicated to promoting the accomplishments of today's quilters. Through its publications and events, AQS strives to honor today's quiltmakers and their work and to inspire future creativity and innovation in quiltmaking.

BOOK EDITOR: KATHY DAVIS
GRAPHIC DESIGN: JEFFREY BECK
COVER DESIGN: MICHAEL BUCKINGHAM
QUILT PHOTOGRAPHY: CHARLES R. LYNCH

Additional copies of this book may be ordered from the American Quilter's Society, PO Box 3290, Paducah, KY 42002-3290, or online at www.AmericanQuilter.com.

Text © 2013, Author, Renae Haddadin
Artwork © 2013, American Quilter's Society

American Quilter's Society
P.O. Box 3290 • Paducah, KY 42002-3290
Fax 270-898-1173 • e-mail: orders@AQSquilt.com

Library of Congress Control Number: 2013942804

BEAUTY FROM WITHIN, detail. Full quilt shown on page 66.
OPPOSITE: SEW MANY SWIRLS, detail. Full quilt shown on page 76.

What a fun job!

I have to say how much I cherish the women who accepted me into their Gone to Pieces Quilt Group and cheered me on when I first started longarm quilting. They trusted me with their precious quilt tops as they said, "Do what you think is best." They applauded my efforts and appreciated my work. I learned so much because of their encouragement and free reign.

As I began teaching at venues around the country, I remain thankful for my students who continue to challenge me with their questions and ideas. I love sharing things that I have learned through mistakes and successes. I appreciate each student's enthusiasm and encouragement to write this book. Having the opportunity to meet so many quilters around the world has been an incredible blessing.

The quilt FIESTA MEXICO was a great catalyst for this book. I am so thankful for the incredible design and workmanship talent of Karen Kay Buckley. I'm even more thankful that she trusted that my work would complement hers and gave me free reign. I look forward to making many more quilts together with Karen. Her designs can be found at www.karenkaybuckley.com.

Working with AQS, the editors, and design team has been a complete pleasure. Their vision and design makes the task of writing a book easy.

In 2009, my dear sister and friend, Vicki, joined me in my quilting business. Soon after that my dearest friend, Janene, began working with us also. There is no way I could do my job without these two amazing women standing alongside me and keeping me on task. I can count on Vicki for anything. If I need help, she is the first one there. Janene keeps me on track and helps me see all things from the bright side. People say that the hardest thing about running a small business is finding good employees. Well, at our shop it is more like hanging out with my best friends, so I don't think of it as work! It is not possible for me to thank Vicki and Janene enough for the help they give me.

Absolutely, I must thank my family for all the support they have given me from the first day my first longarm machine arrived. My boys, Zaid, Tarek, and Rami, encourage me in everything I do. They poke fun at me when I get too uptight and they give me their time when I am desperate for help. I couldn't be more proud to call them my sons. My husband, Muhannad, has never failed to be at my side, encouraging me when I feel overwhelmed and helping me when I truly am overwhelmed. I thank God for the blessing he is to me in everything I do.

Lastly, I am thankful to God for the talents He has blessed me with, in addition to what is listed above and all that isn't listed.

CONTENTS

CONTENTS

I love quilting.

I love to see the fibers of the fabric bend under the thread of the stitching, causing ripples that make the motifs look elevated on the surface of the quilt. I love to see the thread forming even stitches. I love to look at a quilt from across the room and see color, shapes, and bold designs. **But what I love most is when I am drawn in closer to the quilt and I see detail.** A quilt that causes me to press in close and wonder, "How did they do that?" is the best kind of quilt! There are many elements that go into making beautiful quilts. There is the quilt top that often includes piecing, appliqué, painting, or some combination of these. This is where much of the quilt's color and design comes from. But we have all heard the saying, "It isn't a quilt until it's quilted." The quilting stitches can make a good quilt top better and a great quilt top extraordinary. This is why it is so important for the quilting stitches to support the designs of the quilt top. Sometimes the quilt top calls for background fillers that are subtle and disappear, enhancing the quilt top without competing for attention. Other times there are open areas that lend themselves to filler designs that are bold, exciting, and eye-catching. It is important to determine what types of background fillers are suitable for which areas. The variety of filler designs is infinite and this book cannot begin to teach you every design. So please, don't think of this book as just a design book. The goals of this book are threefold: First, to help you envision how the different qualities of each filler design will interact with the other elements of a quilt; Second, to enlarge your filler design repertoire with easy-to-follow stitching lines; and Third, to provide many quilt photos as finished examples to stimulate your own pattern ideas and help you imagine how any given filler design will look in your quilts.

> A quilt that causes me to press in close and wonder "how did they do that?" is the best kind of quilt!

Fig. 1

Fig. 2

Three qualities of background fillers that affect how they look in a quilt

Thread Color and Weight

The thread color used in any background filler design has the greatest effect on how that filler design will look in the finished quilt. Thread that matches the fabric will add texture, without becoming the element that catches your eye as seen in this tile block in FIESTA MEXICO (Fig. 1) and background quilting on SEW MANY SWIRLS (Fig. 2).

"...what I love most is when I am drawn in closer to the quilt and I see detail."

FILLER QUALITIES

Thread saturation in highly-contrasting thread can completely change the look of a quilt as shown in A Brown Tradition (Fig. 3), Sugar & Spice (Fig. 4), and in Fiesta Mexico (Figs. 5–6). Figures 3 and 4 show two sides of the stitching. On one side the thread matches and the other side contrasts. Note how different the two effects are. Since the addition of contrasting thread will become a noticeable design element, it is important to imagine that addition to the finished quilt.

Fig. 3

Fig. 5

Fig. 6

Fig. 4

In HIS LIGHT REFLECTED the colored ring and the eight-pointed center design are examples of how the colored thread becomes a major design (Fig. 7). The large white background areas in this quilt would be a bit boring without the additional color from the filler designs.

When using contrasting thread it is best to define where and how the color saturation will be confined. Make sure that all the areas bordering the thread saturation are enhanced, not obscured, by the added color (Fig. 8). Sometimes a subtle color difference can help differentiate the background from the design, yet still look like it matches. You can see this technique in RADIANCE OF THE SON (Fig. 9). The border designs are stitched with royal thread on royal fabric, but the background stipple is done with black thread. Without pointing this out people may never notice, but it does help the designs show up more.

Fig. 8

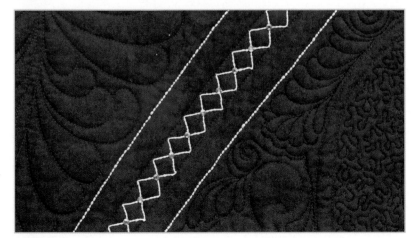

Fig. 9

Fig. 7

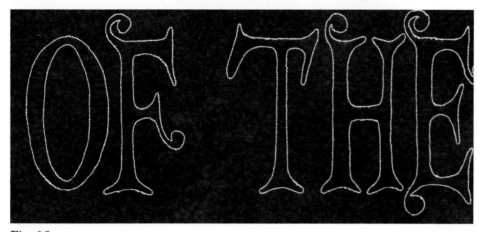

Fig. 10

In addition to the color of thread, the thread weight has an effect. Heavier thread will make more of a statement than thin thread. Outlining designs with heavy contrasting thread is like adding an exclamation point at the end of a sentence! Notice the strong, stitching lines created by using heavy thread in figure 10, figure 11 (thread shown in purple), and figure 12 (heavy thread shown in yellow). However, not all designs can be stitched with heavy thread. Very small designs like the swirling feathers in GOLDEN SNOWFLAKE (Fig. 13) must be stitched with a very fine thread like YLI Silk #100.

Fig. 11

Fig. 12

...the variety of filler designs is infinite.

Fig. 13

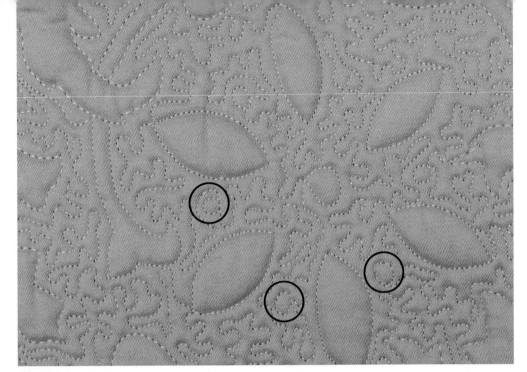

Fig. 14

Filler Scale vs. Motifs

There must be a noticeable distinction between the design size of the motif and the background filler. If they are similar in scale the motif may get lost in the busyness of the background filler design. Notice that the circles in the design in figure 14 are too similar to the background stipple in scale. The circles are obscured by the filler design. Contrast these with the circles in figure 15 where the filler design next to the circles is much smaller than the circles themselves and the circles are accentuated.

Fig. 15

Filler Design Complexity

Motif designs with intricate detail often lose their beauty if they are overpowered by a background (Fig. 16a). This is a great negative example of how busy stitching around an intricate motif causes the motif to be lost. Even beautiful fillers can ruin a quilt when used improperly. The simplest way to know if that might happen to a motif is to look at it from across the room to see if it can hold its ground. Filler designs with dense, even patterns will be more complementary for busy parts of the quilt like the background of figure 17. Pebbles are usually a very subtle background choice. When the designs in the quilt are bold and strong, a busy design can work well, as seen in figure 18.

Figure 16b shows the same motif as figure 16a but with the fillers done in non-contrasting thread. This is a much more appropriate background for an intricate motif design. Non-contrasting thread is used all around the intricate motif to enhance that motif. If another contrasting design is added, you must make sure it doesn't overwhelm the primary design.

Fig. 16a

Fig. 16b

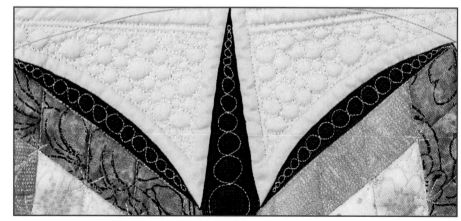

Fig. 17

Fig. 18

Stitching Small Designs

Following are some tips that are helpful for longarm machine users. For quilters who use their domestic machines for quilting I would recommend *Fabulous Feathers & Fillers: Designs & Machine Quilting Techniques*, by Sue Nickels (AQS 2013). Stitching small designs often requires you to move the machine more slowly to achieve the desired accuracy. However, many quilters notice that their longarm machine may wobble a bit when moving slowly. Some steps that may help eliminate the wobbles are:

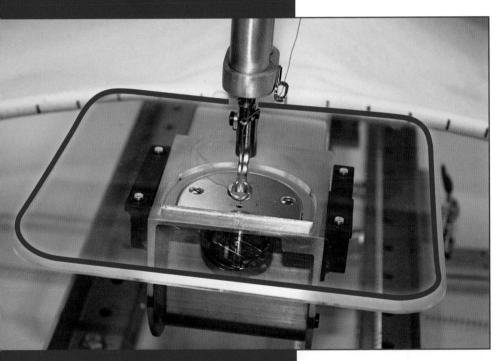

Fig. 19

This larger surface area works as a table to support the quilt. Bouncing is minimized by having the extended base plate in place.

1. Eliminate the gap between the quilt and the throat bed of the machine. If the take-up roller is set very high, the quilt sandwich will bounce and the machine will wobble more. However, if the bar is set too low it will prevent the free movement of the machine. The quilt should just lightly skim the throat plate.

2. Using an extended base plate can help minimize the bouncing (Fig. 19).

3. Keep your elbows close to your body and move the machine with your whole body rather than just your arms. With elbows out like chicken wings, it is much more difficult to control the machine.

4. Stitch in the area closest to you when you stand at the freehand side of the longarm. This is the area where you will have the best control of the machine.

5. If standing, place feet at shoulder's width apart for a steady stance.

6. Clean the carriage, wheels, and table to ensure no thread, lint, or tools are in the way.

7. Secure the machine's cord in a way that will not allow gravity to pull on the machine.

8. Use more stitches per inch to achieve smooth curves on smaller designs. I prefer 15–20 stitches per inch, depending on the design and the thread.

Stitching Order

Dense background fillers cause a quilt to draw in and shrink. Sometimes batting and fabric can migrate around with extensive stitching, causing puckers or distortion. For these reasons it is important to do the background fills after the open areas of the quilt are secured. When working through a quilt on a longarm quilting machine, it is good to stabilize the quilt by stitching the main blocks, borders, and designs first. If there are no blocks it is important to find some way to stabilize the general areas. My goal is to add enough stitching or basting so that no areas larger than an 8"–10" circle remain unsecured. I use my open palm as a guide. I often use stitch in the ditch or outlining designs to secure areas. If there are no reasonable stitching lines I add basting to secure larger areas. Breaking up the open areas locks down the batting and layers of fabric so they do not shift as you work. Sometimes I look for background fillers that shoot off in various directions and I use that quality to break up larger areas into smaller areas. Random columns (Fig. 20) is a good example of a background filler that can work as a stabilizer. Notice that you can travel out beyond the outer edge of the quilt to access new areas without starting and stopping. This stitching will be hidden under the binding.

Fig. 20

Quilting Choices

Before I begin quilting any quilt I make some decisions about how I want it to look. I hang it on a design wall to get that "far away" view. When I look at the whole quilt top I often feel overwhelmed if I think, "How will I fill all that space and enhance the quilt, not overwhelm it?" I have learned that if I try to plan every stitch, I paralyze myself. To prevent this paralysis I try to dissect the quilt in my mind. If I can just concentrate on the big parts for a moment and wait to worry about the smaller areas I prevent "quilt block" in my mind. I think of this as the bones of the quilting. I note which designs or blocks are busy, which areas I want to emphasize, and if there are any sizable blank areas that I will use to place larger motif designs. I decide if I want to add any strong framing features, especially in the border. I choose thread colors and decide if using contrasting thread is suitable. During this overall assessment I pay particular attention to two areas: negative spaces that I want to show up and large areas that would look better broken up.

"I have learned that if I try to plan every stitch, I paralyze myself."

Negative Spaces

When filling background areas on a quilt it is important to notice which elements of the quilt catch your eye. Often the areas that are NOT quilted jump out and show up. This is called the negative space—the area that is left unquilted (Figs. 21–23). Successful motifs are often larger open designs that seem to poof out because the background fillers flatten the batting around them. The area where the stitching is dense often disappears into the elements of the quilt. These areas are typically planned before I begin quilting. Often I do a test stitchout to make sure I like the way it looks before I spend hours on the quilting.

"...it is important to notice which elements of the quilt catch your eye."

Fig. 21

Fig. 22

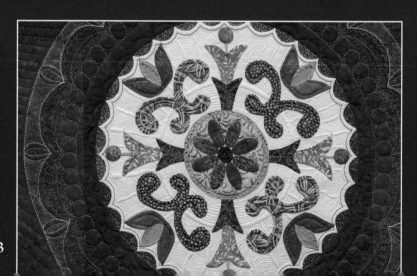

Fig. 23

Fig. 24

Fig. 25

Fig. 26

Breaking Up Large Spaces

After I have the larger motifs planned out, I decide if there are any other areas that need to be broken up into smaller areas or designs that would be enhanced by any frames. These frames are marked, if necessary, ahead of time. Then I can begin the quilting.

Since the first thing I do is stabilize the quilt, I use this time to imagine, touch, and dream as I quilt. I often doodle background fillers on the quilt with a Marvy® Marker (an air-erasable pen). While stitching the planned quilting designs, I usually develop a pretty good plan for the remaining parts of the quilt. Since the bones of the quilt have been decided, I do not feel so overwhelmed as I begin to look at small areas. The small areas always seem to work themselves out. I'm sure that all quilters have different strategies, but this seems to work for me.

A NOTE ABOUT FRAMES: Many designs are linear in their stitching sequence. I use these types of designs to fill a flower's stem, leaf, sashing, or channel such as a frame. Typically they start at one end and travel to the opposite end of a long, narrow space. I keep these types of designs in mind as I add in my frames as in figures 24–26.

Stitching Filler Designs

There is an infinite number of designs suitable to fill up background spaces. They follow a stitching path that wanders around, meshes together, and fills nooks and crannies. These are the designs that are stitched last in the quilting process. These are the parts of the quilt that I haven't planned out from the beginning. These designs are the focus of this book; by understanding their effect on the total quilt, they can be used most effectively.

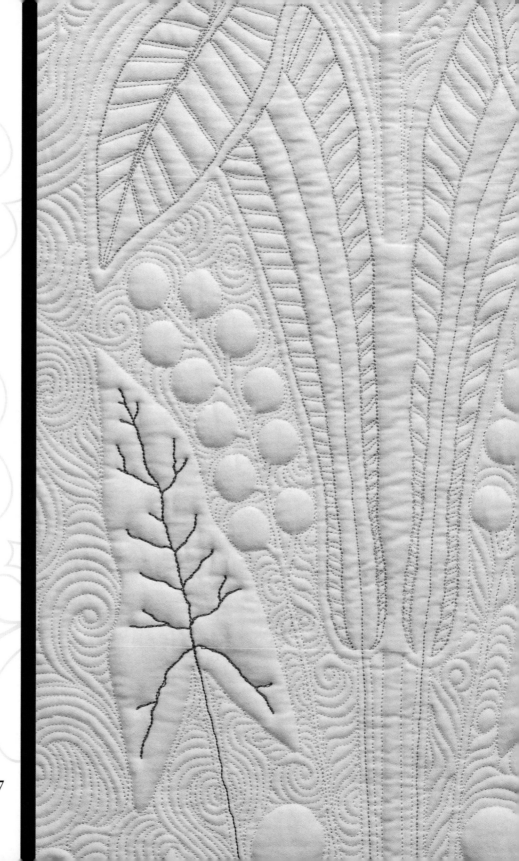

Fig. 27

Designs

Simple Basics

When using any of these basic filler designs, make sure to choose your thread color, scale, and complexity to suit your quilt. Notice that varying the elements will give you a more even, visually pleasing look. Notice in the photos that nearly any design (basic stipple, square spiral, and curls) looks better when there is variation in the design direction and orientation.

In figure 28, the variation in the stitches on the left side give a much more visually appealing look than on the right side, which has no variation and leads to unattractive rows.

...any design looks better when there is variation in the design direction...

Fig. 28

Basic Stipple

The basic stipple is a great filler. Fancy designs
come and go but this is the original stipple. It fills
the background with a dense and even design. By
stitching out into the middle of the open space and
then winding back to fill up the remaining space,
you will stabilize the larger open area. By stitching
a dense and even stipple in a contrasting thread
color, the motif that remains unquilted will stand
out with oomph.

*Fancy designs come and go
but this is the original stipple.*

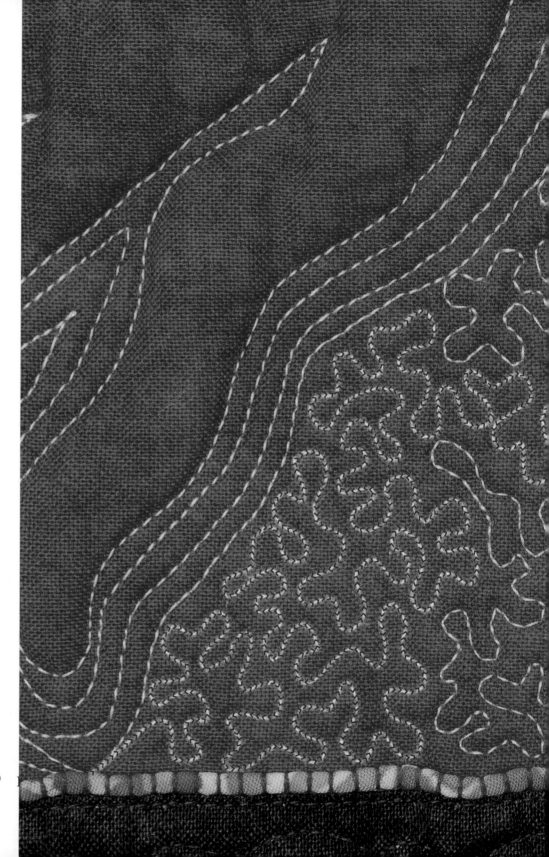

Fig. 29

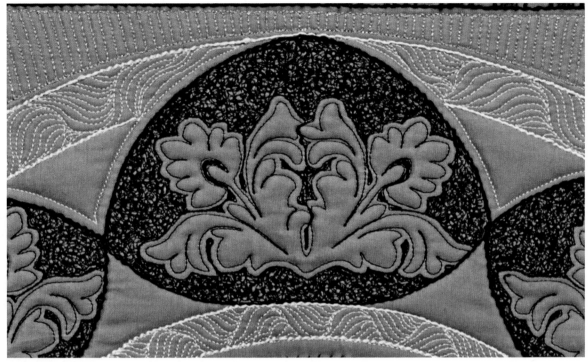

Fig. 30

Blackout

Blackout is used to saturate an area almost completely with thread. In these examples you can see how it completely changes the color. It causes the negative space to stand out clearly in figure 30. It gives the red circle a scalloped edge in figure 31.

Fig. 31

Fig. 32

Worms Filler

In Sew Many Swirls, the cream thread on the cream background forms subtle smooth texture. When stitching this design, just wander with the thread out and about, then echo this wandering thread. Break out and wander some more until you begin to echo again. Let the break-out wandering be balanced with the echoing (Fig. 32).

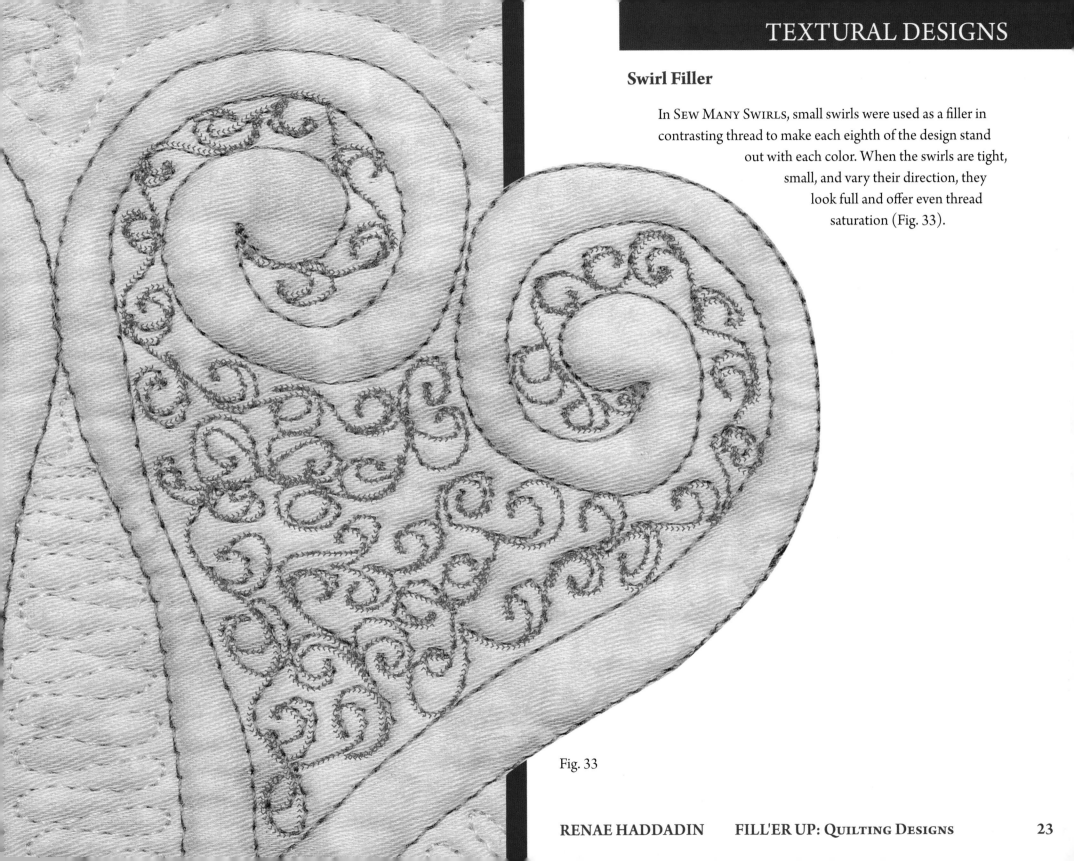

Swirl Filler

In SEW MANY SWIRLS, small swirls were used as a filler in contrasting thread to make each eighth of the design stand out with each color. When the swirls are tight, small, and vary their direction, they look full and offer even thread saturation (Fig. 33).

Fig. 33

Columns of Arcs

Columns are created and then filled with arcs. It is easiest to begin by defining the outer perimeter, and then create the columns and fill them with the arcs. It is often useful to travel along the outer perimeter stitching line. By making a round circle shape (shown in red) and bringing the point of the direction change in deep along the column, this design creates a nice curvy wave that is easy to stitch. This design can create a subtle radiating effect (Fig. 34).

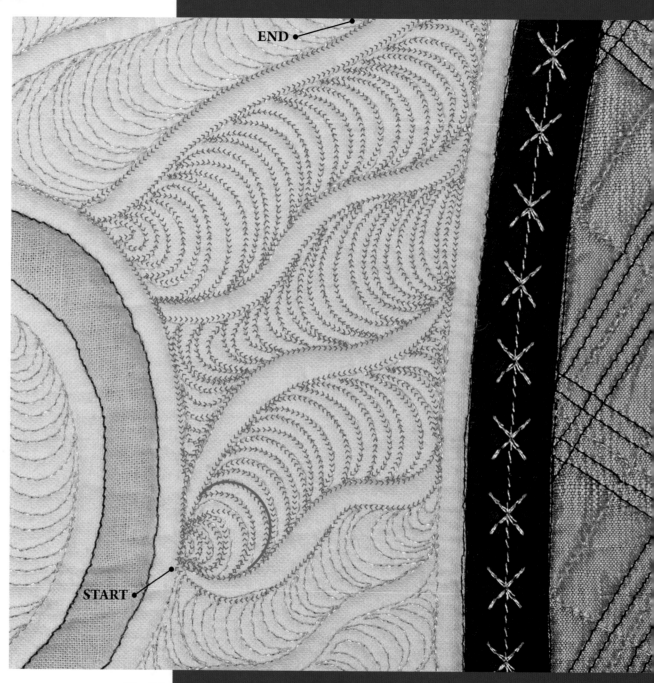

Fig. 34

> "Sometimes you may find yourself boxed into a corner..."

Fig. 35

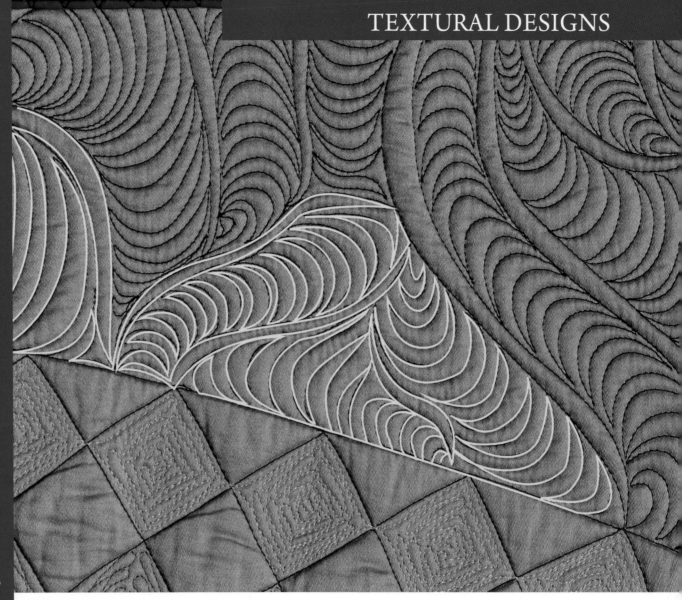

Random Columns of Arcs

This design can be used to stabilize a larger open area by having each column shoot out in various directions. The arcs will naturally vary in their direction creating a nice texture. Sometimes you may find yourself boxed into a corner with your stitching. You can either double-stitch on a previous stitching line or stop and start in a new location (Fig. 35).

Fig. 36

Repeating Arcs

Repeating arcs, as shown in FIESTA MEXICO, will create some areas of thread buildup where many arcs meet forming undulating lines. (In figure 36, repeating arcs are shown in purple). Make sure that the shape of these lines is pleasing. This design can be used to create very dense thread coverage. When done in contrasting thread, the unquilted area will really show up.

"This design can be used to create very dense thread coverage."

"Make sure all the empty areas between circles are filled with echoes."

Fig. 37

Mussels

Mussels are stitched by starting with a circle and echoing the circle with concentric circles. The trick to having this filler look even is to make sure all the empty areas between circles are filled in with echoes. Double-stitch along previously stitched mussels to travel as needed. Vary the number of echoes for variety. Notice these are closed circles, not swirls (Fig. 37).

"...avoid double-stitching and embrace the pointy direction changes."

Fig. 38

Curls

For this nice even filler, avoid double-stitching and embrace the pointy direction changes. Try to keep the distance between the echoes consistent so that the thread saturation is applied evenly and this design will disappear nicely into any background. Change the direction of the curls to add variety (Fig. 38).

Random Greek Key

These randomly sized square spirals move in and out across the quilt top. This filler covers a large, irregular area very nicely. The density of the stitching is very even, making it great filler for many areas. Watch to make sure you always leave an escape route as you enter into a square by leaving the gap between stitching lines two times the width you want it to be when you are finished. Notice that adding in triangular shapes and odd direction changes adds to the interest and makes it easy to move around any kind of obstruction in the quilt top (Fig. 39).

"...make sure you always leave an escape route as you enter into a square..."

Fig. 39

Pearls

This design is very effective in filling any area. Notice that the design can wander around anything. It is easy to use previously stitched pebbles as traveling lines to move to any unquilted area. This makes starts and stops unnecessary (Fig. 40).

"This makes starts and stops unnecessary"

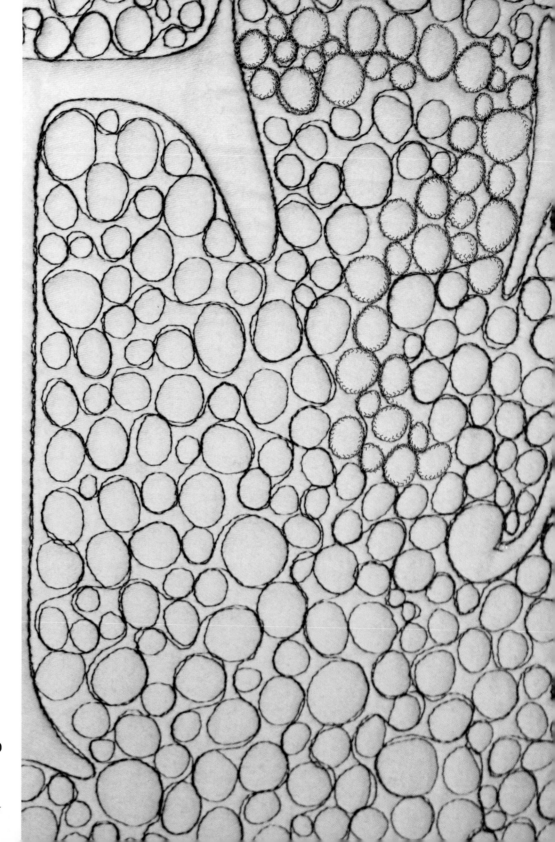

Fig. 40

String of Pearls

These pearls fill channels very nicely. They are stitched with several consecutive "s" shapes that form a half circle, filling the channel in one direction, and then return in the same channel to complete the other side of each half circle (Fig. 41).

"These pearls fill channels very nicely."

Fig. 41

Fire

Fire, shown in red in densely saturated form, is created by zigzagging with a vertical orientation (Fig. 42).

Fire with Leaping Flames

Fire with leaping flames, shown in blue, is created by adding a few swirls and flames with height to the fire (Fig. 42).

Fig. 42

"Fire...is created by zigzagging with a vertical orientation."

Fig. 43

Water

This design is created with softly undulating waves that emulate ripples. Avoid any straight lines while traveling across the quilt in a fairly horizontal direction. Leave open areas to be filled in as the stitches zigzag back and forth across the quilt with smooth direction changes. Notice this design is very similar to fire but the points are smooth and the design is horizontal rather than vertical. Using a subtle variegated thread color can be quite effective (Fig. 43).

This design is created with softly undulating waves...

Fig. 44

Bark

Bark is stitched in much the same way as fire or water, with the addition of some knotty swirls and horizontal orientation. Nature has a way of repeating the same shapes over and over (Fig. 44).

"Nature has a way of repeating the same shapes over and over."

Flagstone or Cracked Sand

This design is formed by stitching a jagged line that wanders over the surface. To form each individual stone, randomly add a jagged hook that juts off the primary stitching line and cordons off an area. Imagine that the stitching line delineates the mortar between each stone. This design requires no double-stitching (Fig. 45).

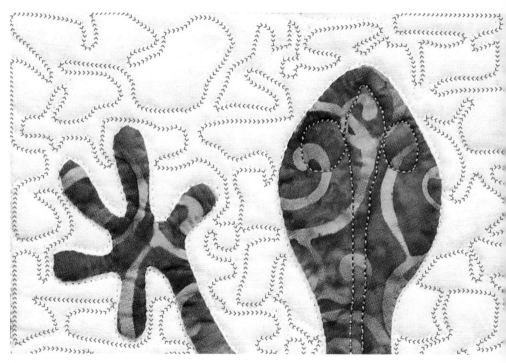

Fig. 45

...the stitching line delineates the mortar between each stone.

Leaves

There are two leaf options shown in figure 46. Both options give a subtle movement to the leaves. They work well on stems since they have a linear movement.

Fig. 46 (right) and detail (above)

More Leaves

Since leaves just scream for a natural texture, more variations are included. The stitching shown above is from the back of the quilt. The green thread actually matches the leaves. See other leaf designs in figure 47.

Fig. 47

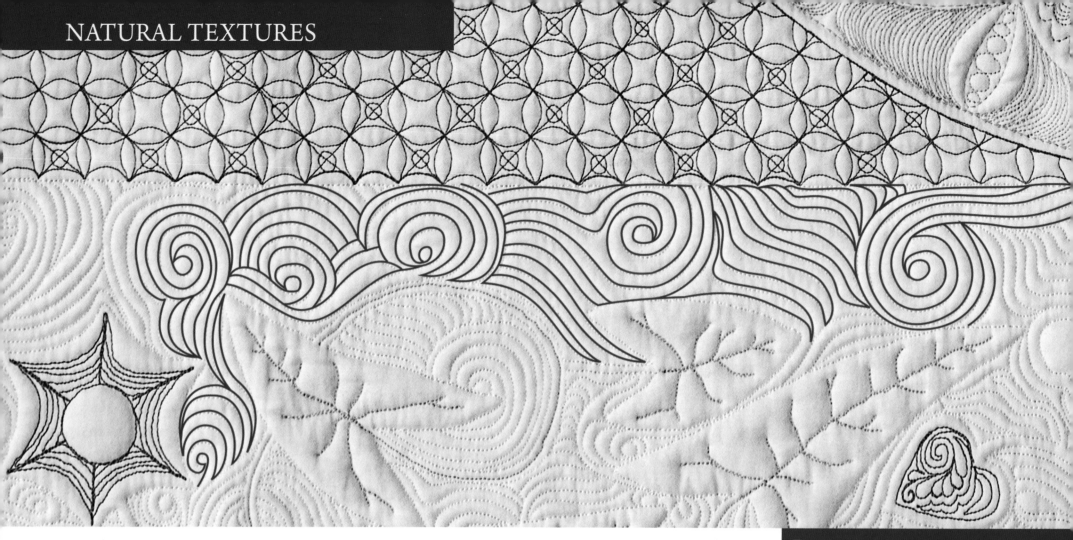

Fig. 48

Flowing Hair

Imagine tufts of curling, waving hair blending together (Fig. 48). This design is graceful and soft and can move easily to fill any area. The stitching line, shown in blue, can travel along previously stitched lines to move to unquilted areas.

"This design is graceful and soft..."

When stitching smooth curves and straight lines, it is very helpful to use a template with markings to guide the machine's hopping foot. These templates are ¼" thick so that the hopping foot will not "hop" over them and break the template. They have etched lines so they can be lined up with previously stitched lines and all the stitched lines will be evenly spaced (Fig. 49). By holding the template firmly with one hand and guiding the machine with the other, you will be able to keep your lines smooth. Note: it is best to confine this filler design to an area that is smallish (8" x 8"). It can be very tricky to stitch straight lines for a long distance.

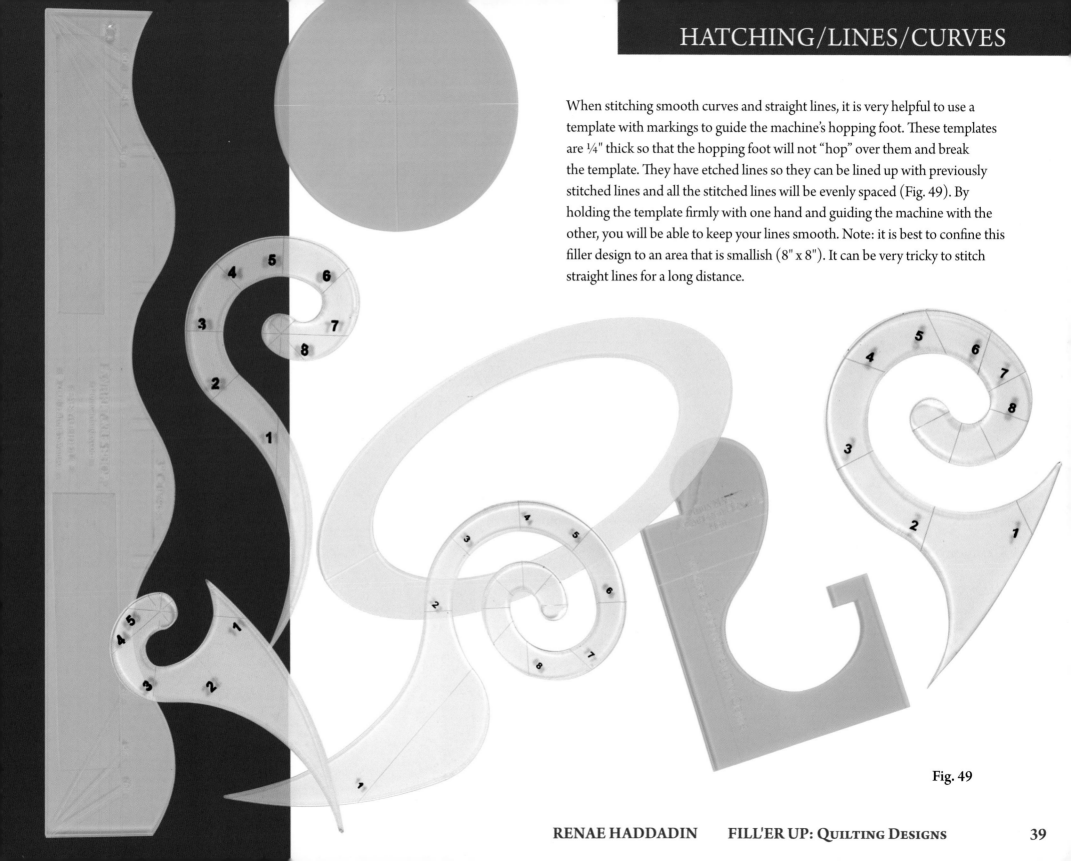

Fig. 49

Fig. 50

Concentric Circles

Concentric circles create a feeling that the design is radiating outward from a central point. The design is very simple and does not overpower (Figs. 50–51).

Fig. 51

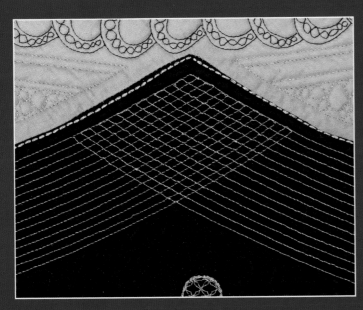

Fig. 52

Fig. 53

Fig. 54

Repeated Curves

Repeated curves form miniature curved crosshatching. These curves can be close together as seen in GOLDEN SNOWFLAKE (Fig. 52), or a bit further apart like in BEAUTY FROM WITHIN (Fig. 53).

This technique is done by outlining the area first, then stitching the curves by moving from one side to the other along the edge of a template (Fig 54). Then move the template over a small increment and stitch back again until the curves are completed in one direction, shown in red. Then do the same thing in the other direction, shown in green in figure 52.

The curves do not need to cross over each other to be beautiful. In FIESTA MEXICO (Fig. 55) the curves are done in silver thread and add both texture and sparkle to the vase.

Fig. 55

Fig. 56 An example of miniature crosshatching

Miniature Crosshatching

This is a great background for a traditional quilt that will not overpower the designs in the quilt top. Here in figure 56, the design adds texture and variety to the larger open space. By using a template to guide the stitching lines, they will be straight and evenly spaced. The stitching sequence begins at one side and goes back and forth in parallel lines (like the blue). Then stitch the lines that are at a 90-degree angle in the same fashion.

"...the design adds texture and variety to the larger open space."

Fig. 57

Fig. 58

Argyle

Argyle spacing can add more interest. It takes a bit more planning to figure out how to stitch lines with more and then less space, but the effect can be worth the effort. The stitching sequence is the same as miniature crosshatching (Fig. 57) where the thread is all the same. Figure 58 shows a regular crosshatching design stitched in silver thread, then the additional lines are added in black thread. In figure 59, argyle clearly adds interest to the pot.

"It takes a bit more planning... but the effect can be worth the effort."

Fig. 59

Fig. 60

Fig. 61

Simple Straight Lines

In Golden Snowflake (Fig. 60) the small area of simple lines fills an area that mimics the shape of the border design, enhancing that shape. Notice that even contrasting thread doesn't overwhelm the design because the lines are so simple and dense.

You can see in figure 60 that simple straight lines can often frame or emphasize a part of the quilt. In Fiesta Mexico (Figs. 61–62), these flowers become the center of attention when the frames of simple lines are added.

Fig. 62

Radiating Lines

Radiating lines are a great effect to highlight a center design. An example can be seen in figures 63–64. Avoid bringing the radiating line all the way to the center area. This causes too much thread buildup as the lines get closer together. Mark the lines prior to stitching them so that it is easy to maintain even spacing. I use Renae's Miniray to do this marking.

Fig. 64

"...a great effect to highlight a center design."

Fig. 63

GRID WORK

Basic Curves

Basic curves are stitched in a continuous fashion by following the red arrows vertically, and continuing with the blue arrows horizontally. The easiest way to stitch basic curves is to draw a grid in the desired size to serve as registration lines (Fig. 64). Then stitch a serpentine path making sure the stitching crosses at the grid-line intersections (circled in green). When all the serpentine lines are complete it will form a design that looks like interlocking circles (Fig. 65).

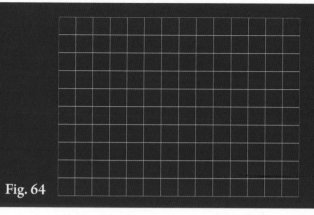

Fig. 64

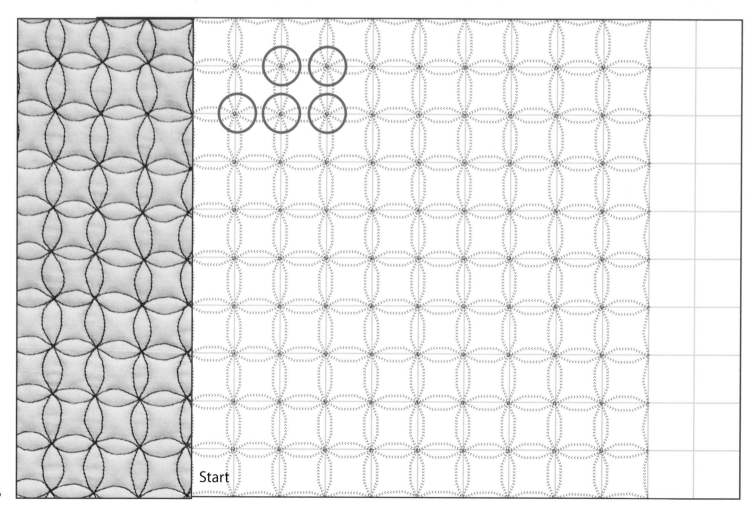

Start

Fig. 65

Basic Curve Variation 1

A basic curve variation can be created by adding any additional filler to the grid of rings. The center areas can be filled as you move diagonally with the stitching as in figure 66.

A variety of filler stitches can be used to fill in every other center area for a beautiful effect. Double-stitch along the outer edge to get to the next row.

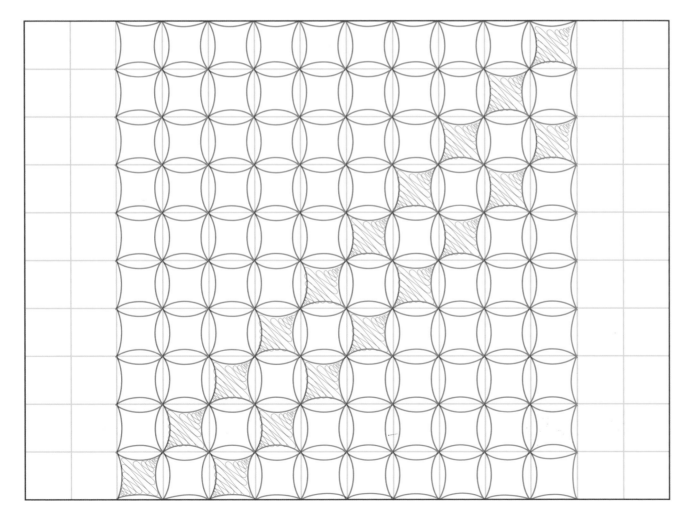

Fig. 66

"A variety of filler stitches can be used to fill in every other center area for a beautiful effect."

Basic Curve Variation 2

The ring sections can be filled as shown in figure 67.

To stitch this variation, add a string of pearls in each melon shape. If you stitch a waving line from one side to the other and then repeat that waving line in reverse, you will have a string of pearls filling the melons.

Move over to the next row of melons and do it again!

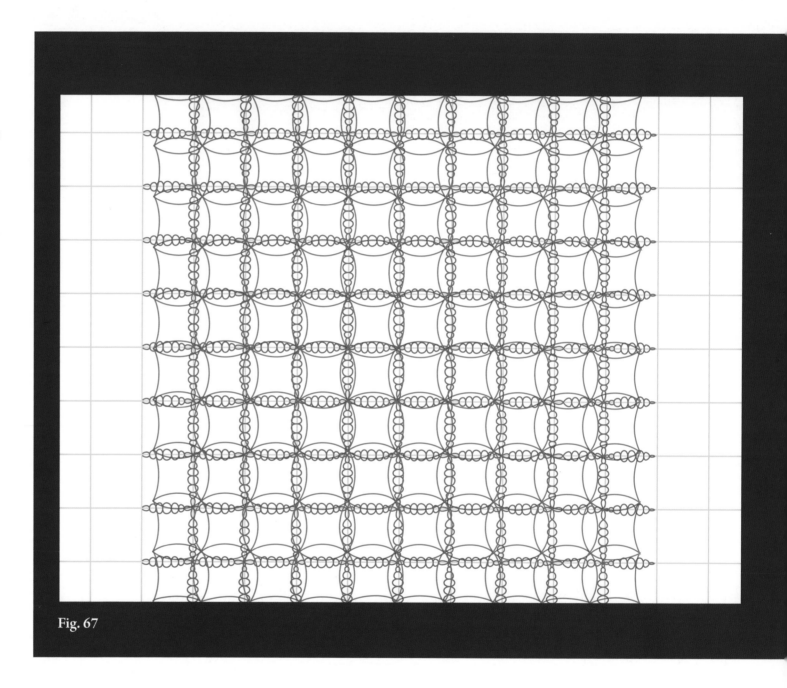

Fig. 67

Basic Curve Variation 3

Figure 68 shows an apple-core design.

It is created by stitching half of the curved lines in the basic design.

Stitch following the pink curved lines of one color. This is a continuous wavy line that will hit each intersection of the drawn grid. Then stitch the green lines in the same fashion. Notice that each wavy line has the curve facing the opposite way as the next wavy line to create the thin, then wide apple-core design.

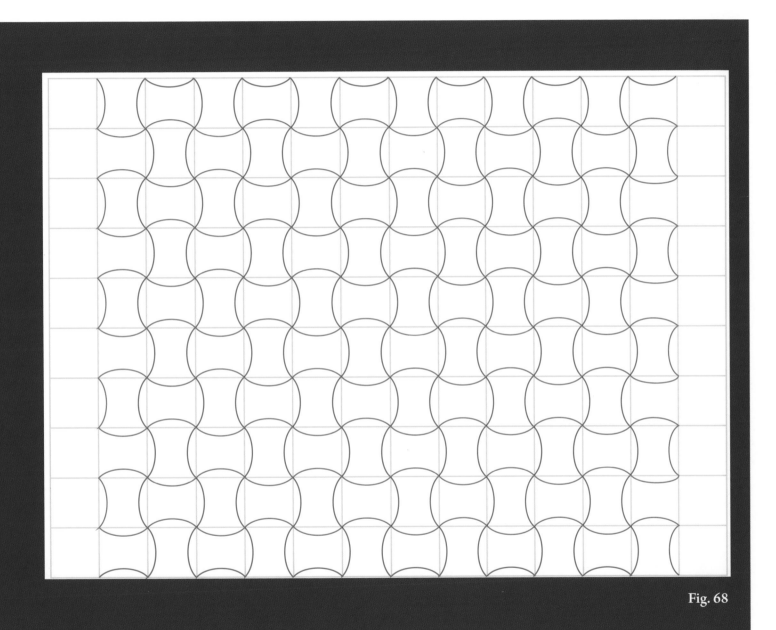

Fig. 68

Basic Curve Variation 4

Variation 4 (Fig. 69) uses the same wavy lines as variation 3 but they are placed a bit differently.

Stitch following the curved lines of one color. This is a continuous wavy line that will hit each intersection of the drawn grid. Then stitch the green lines in the same fashion. Notice that the wavy lines are the same as variation 3 but they are offset by one square.

Make sure you wave the right way to get the look you want.

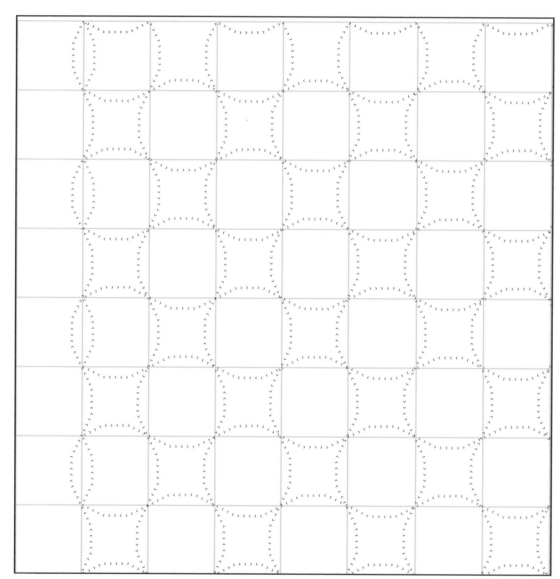

Fig. 69

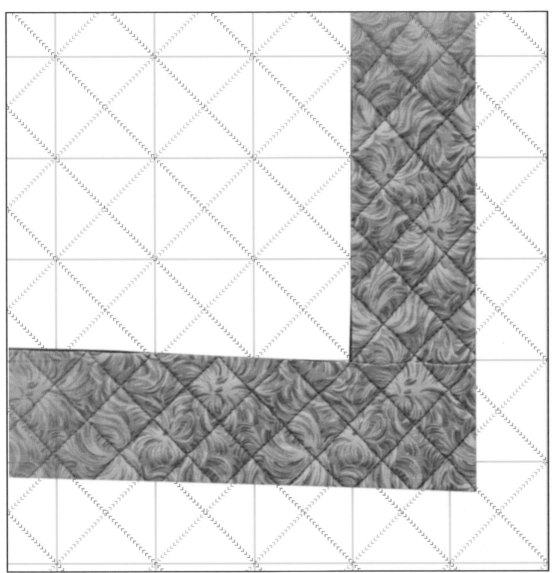

Fig. 70

Basic Square Grid

This is basic crosshatching. It can be done in any shaped area by traveling along the perimeter to the next line as shown in the miniature crosshatch diagram (Fig. 70). Start your first pass on the orange lines, and then stitch the green lines.

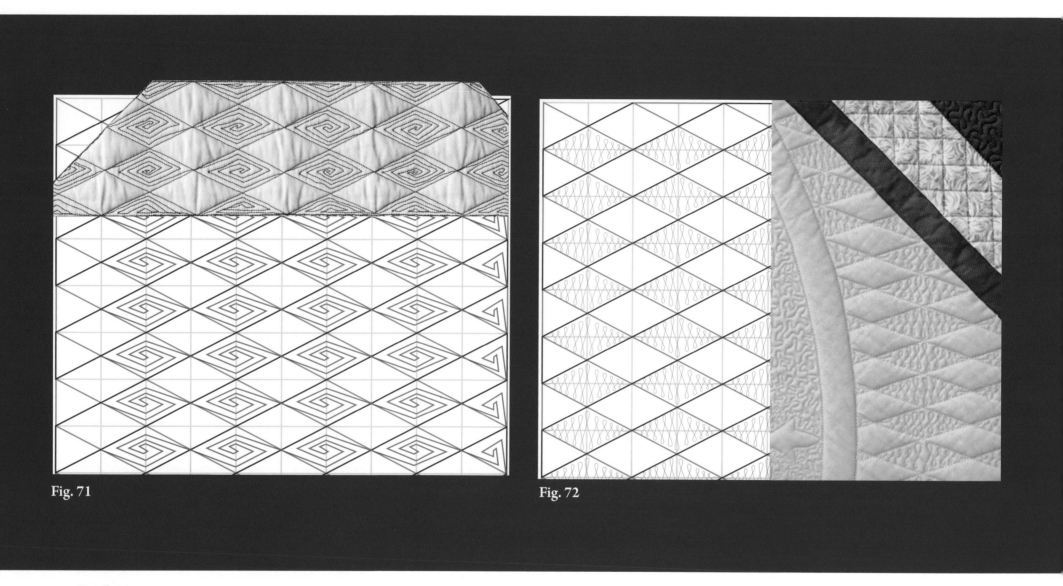

Fig. 71

Fig. 72

Grid 1

Following the yellow grid guidelines, stitch all the green lines, then the blue ones. Add any filler design in every other diamond to create a checkerboard effect. By changing the angle of the lines, it will create diamonds. By filling diamonds with any other filler design, a checkerboard will be formed (Figs. 71–72).

Grid 2

By adding stars at the intersection of the lines, a new pattern is formed (Fig. 73).

Using the yellow grid guidelines , stitch all the green lines , then the orange ones. Stars can be added at each intersection for more interest.

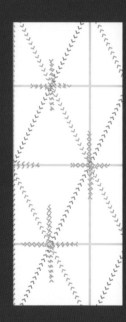

Fig. 73

Basic Clamshells

Basic Clamshells are made by making half ovals or circles between intersections on a marked grid (Fig. 74).

Basic Clamshell Variation 1–3

Variations are easy to create by adding something to the pattern. Notice that the addition can be at the valley of the clamshell intersection going up (Figs. 75–76) or down (Fig. 77).

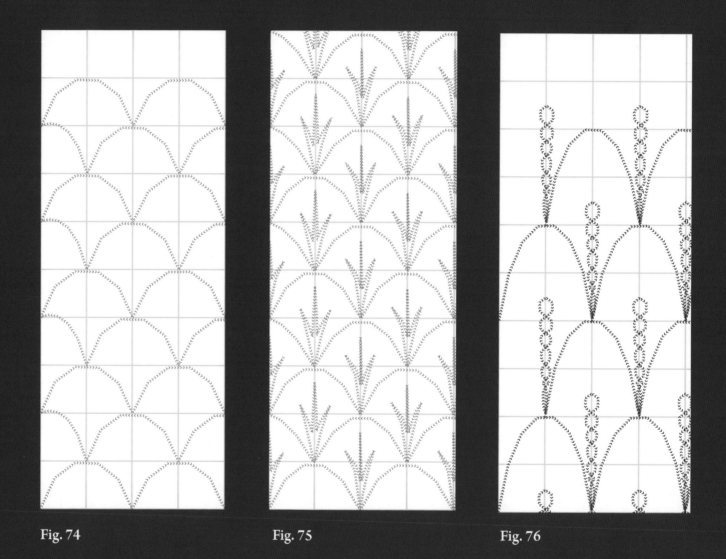

Fig. 74   Fig. 75   Fig. 76

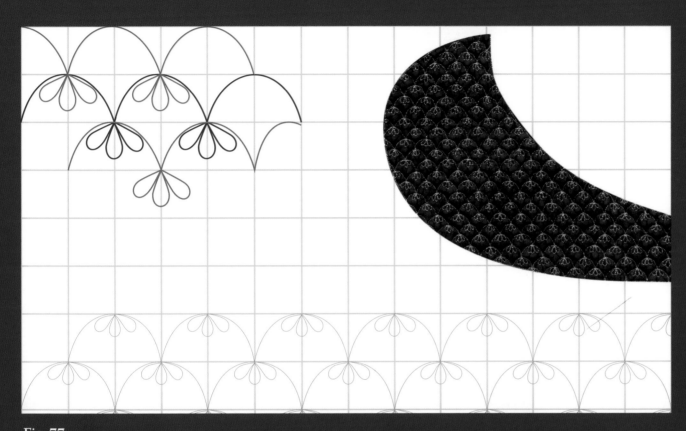

Stitch the clamshell. At the valley drop down into the previous clamshell, insert a teardrop in the center, then another one on each side. Continue with the next clamshell.

Fig. 77

"The possible variations to the basic clamshell are limitless."

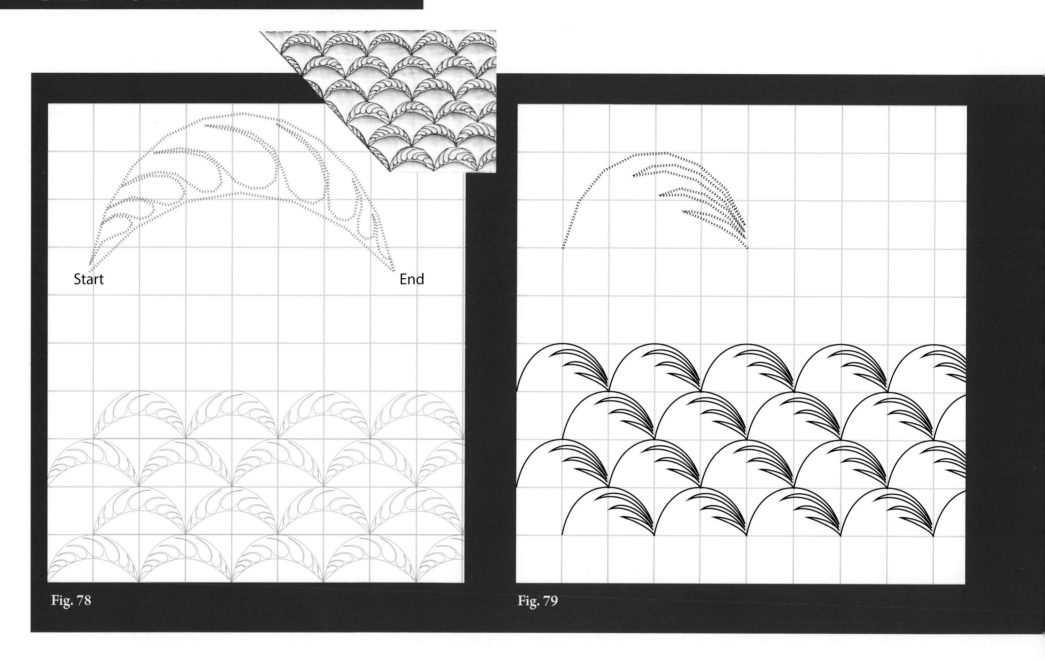

Fig. 78

Fig. 79

Start   End

Basic Clamshell Variation 4–5

These variations can go into the clamshell from the sides as shown in figures 78–79.

Feathers & Swirls

Feathers and swirls can be great fillers for various areas. There are many places that look fantastic with flowing feathers. They can adorn flowers, hearts, empty corners, or wide-open spaces. Of all the quilting designs, feathers and their variations are my personal favorites. I am usually looking for places where I can squeeze them in (Fig. 80).

"...feathers and their variations are my personal favorites."

Fig. 80

Feather 1

Feather 1 shows how a very even, symmetrical feather can strengthen a frame. In figure 81, there is a frame that breaks up a very large border area. This border is too large and the center section is too small to leave it as a whole open area. The silver cross-hatching strengthens the frame, while the navy feathers fill the space and strengthen the frame. This nicely divides the area.

Notice the stitching sequence of these feathers. There is double-stitching along the short curved section (marked in pink) rather than along the longer section (marked in yellow). I have found that it is easier for me to bend and curve my feathers into graceful shapes by using this stitching sequence. It takes a bit of practice to master but it is worth the effort.

NOTE: The double-stitching in figure 81 shows the second stitching line is near the previous stitching line. This is just for visual clarity in the diagram. The second stitching is best when it is directly over the first stitching.

Fig. 81

Feather 2

Feather 2 is similar to Feather 1 but the length of the feathers varies to fill the entire space. The matching thread, shown in pink, makes this a beautiful filler design that is understated and graceful to match the bend of the leaves.

It takes a bit of practice to learn to curve and bend feathers. Notice how using combinations of long and short feather fronds makes it possible for the strand of feathers to flow gracefully over the quilt (Fig. 82).

"This is a beautiful filler design that is understated and graceful...."

Fig. 82

Feather 3

Feather 3 uses the same basic feather used in Feather 1 in an "s" shape. Nesting several "s" shapes together forms a beautiful, winding vine of feathers. The sequence to stitching each "s" shape in a continuous line is to start with the "s" shaped line, feather up the side, stitch the second "s" near the first, then feather up that remaining side. Each feathered "s" shape is stitched as one unit. Stitch as many units as necessary to fill your space (Fig. 83).

"...a beautiful winding vine of feathers."

Fig. 83

Fig. 84

Feather 4

Feather 4 uses the same bending, flowing feathers as figure 83 to wind and fill all the spaces between appliquéd flowers (shown in pink and blue lines). Because the scale is smaller, they are able to fit into the tiniest crevices. Notice on this design there is no spine for the feathers (Fig. 84).

NOTE: These feather plumes have long thin fronds that pull back into each other forming a faux spine. This is why I am able to bend and curve them.

Once I have a very long feather frond (shown in purple), I will use that as a spine to build feather fronds in the other direction.

The pink highlighted stitches are all one continuous feather.

The brown highlighted stitches are the beginning of a second group of feathers.

NOTE: This is shown from the back side of Fiesta Mexico for clarity.

Feather 5

Feather 5 takes the feather concept just a bit farther. I added in some swirls to use as spines and build feather fronds upon. Use the long feather fronds as spines, also. Echo the shapes to move to unquilted areas.

This combination has no right-side up or upside down. Keep the feathers moving in various directions to maintain the appeal (Fig. 85).

"Keep the feathers moving in various directions..."

Fig. 85

Feather 6

Feather 6 is a combination of many designs to fill an entire wedding dress skirt. There are areas of feathers, pebbles, wacky crosshatching, echoing, mussels, and more. In this case there were no major motifs that I was concerned might be overpowered. My goal was to fill space and saturate the creamy satin with gold thread (Fig. 86).

Fig. 86

FIESTA MEXICO

This quilt was the catalyst for writing this book.

With the nonsymmetrical setting of the blocks it seemed fitting to include the many different designs in the quilting. As I began to contemplate all the fun designs I planned to use on this quilt, I realized that they would fill a book.

"This quilt was the catalyst for writing this book."

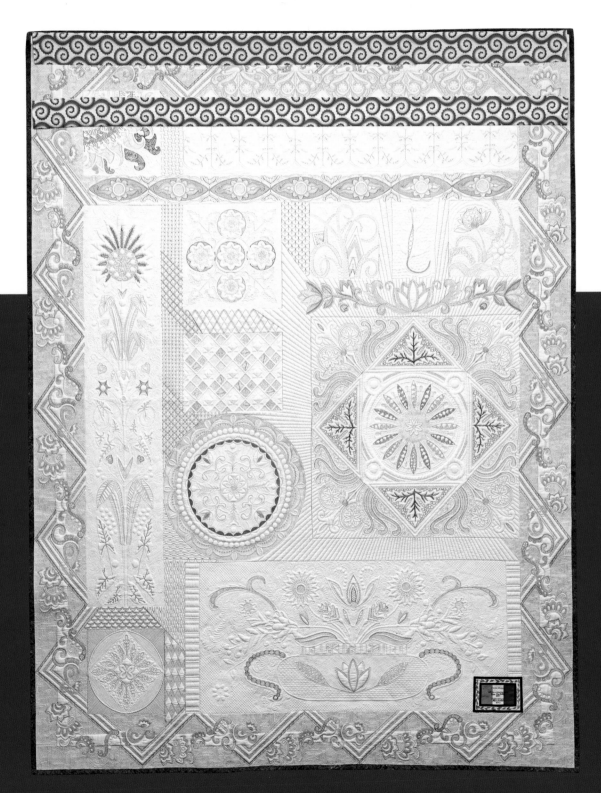

Fiesta Mexico

Reverse side

BEAUTY FROM WITHIN

Many of my quilts are based on Bible studies I was doing at the time they are created. Often women are taught by our society that beauty is outside, but I designed this quilt around shadow embroidery where the color and beauty come from the inside, like the Bible teaches.

"Color and beauty come from the inside, like the Bible teaches."

CARIBBEAN BLUE

This bright wallhanging was made after a Caribbean cruise to celebrate the fun colors and clear water of the area. Made as a sample using my designing techniques, it hangs in the hallway to cheer up anyone in the house.

"...made to celebrate the fun colors and clear water..."

GOLDEN SNOWFLAKE

This miniature quilt was a fun experiment to try some computerized embroidery and computerized quilting designed by JoAnn Hoffman. The center embroidery was stitched on batiste, set into the fabric, and then quilting was added. At least eight different threads were used to create depth and variety.

"...a fun experiment..."

HIS LIGHT REFLECTED

I have always loved shading colors using fabrics. I really enjoyed shopping for just the right fabrics to create this color wheel.

"I have always loved shading colors using fabrics."

RADIANCE OF THE SON

Based on a sermon series, this quilt was made as a gift to my church. It is full of symbolism based on Bible verses. This quilt hangs in the church's sanctuary.

"full of symbolism based on Bible verses..."

A BROWN TRADITION

I made this quilt to match the colors in my bedroom. While making it, I learned a great deal about size and scale of quilting designs.

"While making this quilt, I learned a great deal about size and scale..."

RING AROUND THE ROSIE

This quilt was my first attempt at making a two-sided quilt. Matching up the embroidery on the front and the back so that the quilting was complementary on both sides was a great challenge.

I liked it enough to do it again when I made SUGAR AND SPICE (pg. 74).

"...my first attempt at making a two-sided quilt..."

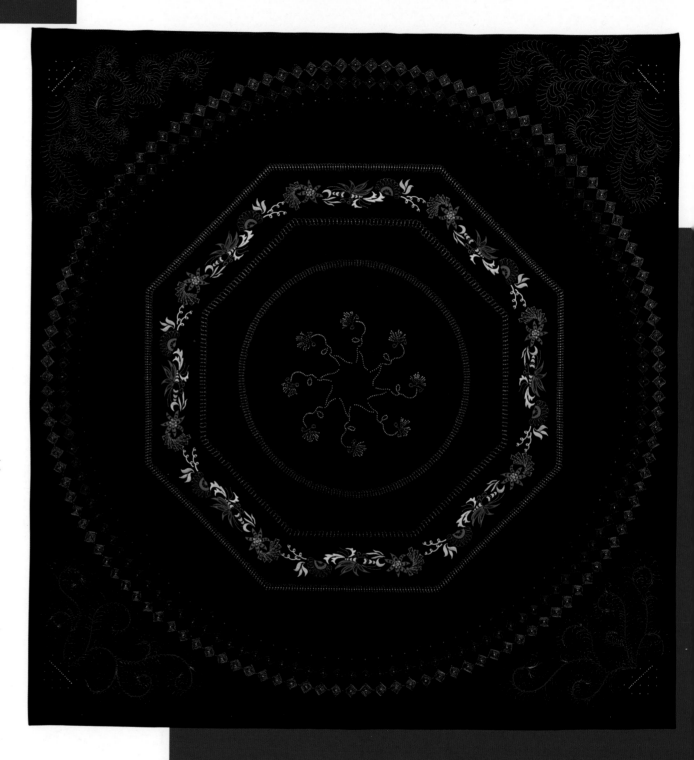

Ring Around the Rosie

Reverse side

SUGAR & SPICE

This quilt was my second attempt at a two-sided quilt. The embroidery designs were created to complement the opposite side. The quilting is the same color on both sides, but looks very different on the black vs. white fabric.

"...the embroidery designs complement the opposite side..."

SUGAR & SPICE

REVERSE SIDE

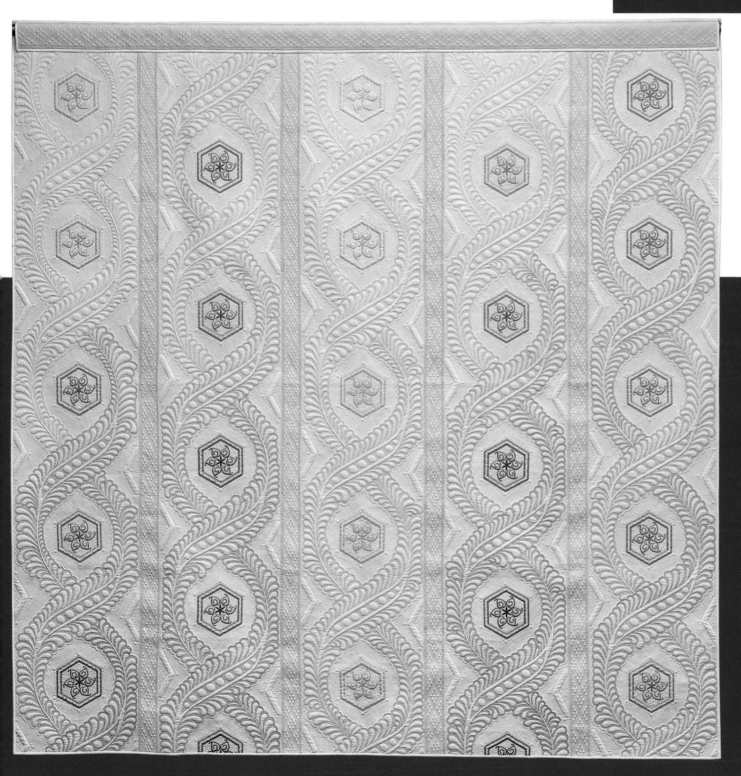

SEW MANY SWIRLS

When I was just getting my longarm business going I thought that if I made a quilt that was well quilted and entered it into quilt shows, it would help me enlarge my customer base. This was my first attempt at heirloom/show-type quilting.

"This was my first attempt at heirloom/show-type quilting."

BELLE FOR A DAY

I was very honored to be trusted to make my daughter-in-law's wedding dress. Brittany always dreamed of having a dress like "Belle" in *Beauty and the Beast*.

She wanted a gold wedding dress so a tremendous amount of gold thread was used to "gild" the fabric. Brittany was truly "Belle" for a Day!

"...Brittany always dreamed of having a dress like 'Belle'..."

Photo by Charles Lynch
and modeled by Anna Riddle

Renae began longarm quilting in 2002 when she started her home-based business. With her youngest child in first grade and the need for some additional income, she decided that quilting would not only be fun, it would fit into her home life. She quilted for customers for several years, enjoying the art while being able to raise her family. It was a great blending of work and home. As her children grew and needed less mothering, Renae expanded her quilting business and moved to a brick and mortar shop. It seemed fitting that the historic bank building in Old Sandy, Utah, would be home to a vibrant quilting studio.

Renae loves the outdoors and spends a considerable amount of time camping, home renovating, running, and hiking. Time spent running is often her best time to figure out the logistics of how to make her design ideas work. She recently became a grandmother and has quickly adapted to the life of an empty nester.